Testimonials

"An **important, common-sense approach** to business development for associates at every level. Use this checklist to promote a thoughtful marketing discussion and real action."

Eileen Cohen Billinson, Principal at Billinson • Latorre
Former Director of Business Development, Morgan Lewis

"This is **an incredibly useful resource** to get associates on track towards productive, career-long, business development habits."

Bettina Rutherford, Business Development Manager, K&L Gates

"I have used Ross's **highly practical framework** in several firms and **strongly recommend it**. It helps lawyers demystify marketing and business development and take concrete, manageable actions to achieve success on their own terms and according to their own style. I have seen it literally give hope to associates who thought that developing a sustaining legal practice was beyond their ability."

Nathan Darling, Chief Marketing Officer, Beveridge and Diamond
Legal Marketing Associations (LMA) President, 2010

"Ross's Checklist is my go-to for both casual 'stop-by' conversations with associates and formal associate-training programs. With **clear guidelines** for marketing and business development by experience level, this tool is **immensely helpful**. I've had many partners comment on how smart this checklist is, and that they wish they had something like this when they were coming up the ranks."

Jennifer Shankleton, Director of Marketing, Brouse McDowell

"Ross's insightful checklist is a practical guide to marketing yourself at every stage of your career. His book details realistic and attainable marketing and business development activities. I am a fifth-year associate and have been implementing the recommendations for a few years and can already see how they are positioning me to generate business in the future. **I strongly recommend this valuable checklist** to associates at all levels—from first-year lawyers fresh out of school to senior associates who are eligible for partner. Thank you, Ross!"

Randall Borek, Fifth-Year Associate, Murphy & Hourihane

Testimonials

"This book needs to be in the hands of every young associate who wants to have a successful, rewarding legal career. Just follow this practical 'how to' guide to become a top-tier rainmaker in your firm, large or small. The practical links to cogent examples add to the effectiveness and bring it alive for the reader. *This checklist should be a 'best seller.'"*

Ron Henry, Law Firm Consultant, The Garver Group, Inc.
President, Association of Legal Administrators (ALA), 2002-03

*"Ross has turned an intimidating and challenging process into simple, practical, and systematic steps. **I have used his checklist for many years with great success.** He has removed the 'deer in the headlights' moment and crafted something associates can use to see success."*

Aleisha Gravit, Chief Marketing Officer, Akin Gump
LMA President, 2013

*"Practical and engaging, Ross's step-by-step, thoughtful and practical advice helps lawyers succeed. A valuable tool both for associates and their mentors, it **should be in the hands of every lawyer!** It takes the mystery out of developing a book of business."*

Hallie J. Mann, Executive Director, Lawyers Associated Worldwide

*"**Essential reading for every associate at any point in their career!** Every lawyer can use this comprehensive checklist to jumpstart, or build on, their efforts to grow their reputation and successfully achieve their professional goals.* In an industry defined by how your clients and peers speak of you, this checklist holds all the secrets to creating a powerful referral network. **It is marketing nirvana.**"

Nathaniel Slavin, Principal, Wicker Park Group
LMA President, 2007

"A must-read for all associates."

Allan Slagel, Partner, Taft Stettinius & Hollister

THE ULTIMATE LAW FIRM ASSOCIATE'S MARKETING CHECKLIST

The Renowned Step-By-Step, Year-By-Year Process for Lawyers Who Want to Develop Clients.

Third Edition

by
Ross Fishman, JD
CEO
Fishman Marketing, Inc.

Published by Ross Fishman, Highland Park, Illinois
fishmanmarketing.com

ISBN: 978-0-9979676-2-3

Manufactured in the United States

Cover design by Michelle Benjamin

In Memoriam

Ian Turvill
1965-2017

Dad, husband, son, friend, CMO.
Truly, one of the good guys.

Dedication

This book is dedicated to the hard-working **law firm associates** who strive to master a complex and challenging craft. They work long hours for demanding clients, both inside and outside their firms. They graduated into an uncertain economy, in a profession with high billable hours but low client loyalty. Controlling their own book of business is the only professional safety net that exists.

In today's economy, more new law grads are hanging out their own shingle or are asked to find clients swiftly. We recommend these same strategies, just apply them on an expedited time-frame; get out with people and start developing that niche focus immediately.

It is equally dedicated to all the **in-house legal marketers** who toil in the trenches every single day, helping their lawyers and law firms succeed. They're the smartest and most generous professionals I've ever met; I'm blessed to call them my friends.

Above all, it's dedicated to my amazing wife, Kitty, and my four wonderful children—Andrew, Rob, Jonathan, and Elyssa—who make every day a joy.

Book Overview

Marketing's not difficult. Plan, prepare, and execute steadily over time. A little bit every week. *Drip, drip, drip.* Just make sure the things you are doing are the *right* things.

That's what this book is designed to facilitate.

Here's the basic overview:

- Learn to be a great lawyer, emphasizing both technical skills and client service. You can't just bring in the work, you gotta be able to do it too.

- Build your long-term marketing infrastructure, the social media platform and other tools you'll leverage through partnership and beyond.

- Join a local bar association, meet your peers, get active, and build your resume.

- Gradually add more external marketing and networking activities. Build your personal brand.

- Develop a narrow specialty or industry niche in an area you enjoy. Avoid becoming one more generic generalist; seek to dominate something. Focus your marketing on a specialized trade group.

- Look for additional cross-selling opportunities with existing clients.

- As you get more experienced, spend more time out of the office with prospects and referral sources.

That's the big picture; the rest of the book will detail the specific activities. **If you ever have any questions, shoot me an email at ross@fishmanmarketing.com.** I'd be delighted to hear from you.

Table of Contents

Foreword

So it's early 1990 and a young blond man wearing a neat, pinstriped suit walks into my office. I was the newly minted marketing partner at Winston & Strawn. It was a typically cold, damp, dank, and windy winter day in Chicago.

My visitor was Ross Fishman, and my long and largely unproductive day quickly took a turn for the better. The fellow had that spark of personality, ready smile, and gift of gab that define a live wire. I sensed this right from the start.

Ross proved to be an invaluable colleague. It seems that he'd recognized before most of us that common corporate practices like branding, differentiation, and standing apart from the crowd in a commoditized industry apply to the practice of law. He found his life's work: teaching lawyers and law marketers at all levels of experience how to develop and expand business.

Now Ross' wise counsel is in book form and the book is in your hands. Do not put it down! For despite his legal training, his law degree, and bar membership, his writing is clear, concise, free of clichés, and as easy to digest as a chewable vitamin. Anecdotes, examples (both positive and negative), humor, and pathos leap off the pages of this volume. They will help you find clients and their hearts, minds, and wallets. This book is a bargain at twice the price.

I read this book. I laughed. I cried. I lost 10 pounds.

Try it—you'll like it!

Loren A. Wittner

Former Marketing Partner, Winston & Strawn
Phoenix, Arizona

Preface

The law is a challenging, competitive profession; many associates live in a constant state of unease. They want to know how they're doing, how they're comparing to their peers in the firm and across the industry. And the anxiety doesn't go away as they advance through their careers. In fact, it often increases, as they wonder if they're doing everything they can to improve their chance of partnership or autonomy, including developing their own clients.

I regularly see smart, personable, highly motivated senior associates or junior partners who have been working tirelessly on client development for many years, with nothing to show for it. After we sit down and discuss their marketing efforts thus far, it's often obvious to me that the activities they'd been undertaking had little chance of success. I don't want to discourage them, even when I'd like to say, "Yeah, that stuff was never going to work." It's not their fault; they just got bad advice. Or no advice at all.

I vividly remember my years as a litigation associate, receiving at most a few hours of marketing training per year. Eventually, I left the practice of law to market law firms full time, first as a big-firm Marketing Director, then Marketing Partner. There was always a steady stream of associates dropping by my office, hungry for practical, realistic advice and assistance. The guidance they'd received from their bosses and mentors tended toward "Here's what *I* did [i.e., 30 years ago, before the Internet]."

This continues today, with many firms wanting to conduct their marketing training using their successful rainmaking senior partners. The logic is that they *must* know how to do it, because they have a lot of business. It makes sense in theory—but it rarely works in practice.

I've participated in hundreds of law firm marketing training programs and retreats, many of which included presentations by firm rainmakers, only a handful of whom actually offered useful advice.

Candidly, most of these rainmakers have no idea *how* they generated the business. They might *think* they know, but it's just their gut feeling. They know *something* worked, but only rarely what it really was. Further, a lot has changed since a 60-year-old set out to build his or her early practice. Back then, it was a seller's market for legal services. There were no global firms. No legal-outsourcing companies. No Internet or social media. You could hear the clacking of the secretaries' typewriters.

It's hard to credibly offer networking advice to a 30-year-old lawyer when your LinkedIn profile has no text, one connection, and you don't know your password.

Typical associate laments include:

- "What she *really* did was inherit a book of business from a retired partner."

- "[Joe Rainmaker] is charming, funny, and the life of the party; he's out drinking with prospects every night and has a 6 handicap. I'm introverted—his methods are never going to work for me."

- "I'm already billing 1,800 hours. I don't have time to market."

- "She keeps saying, 'Good work is the best marketing.' What, our competitors aren't good lawyers too?"

- "He says he gets clients by 'providing excellent client service,' but his dad is a U.S. Senator!"

- "He made one friend in his whole life, and *that* guy became GC of a big bank and gives him all his legal work. That's not strategy, that's dumb luck."

So without sufficient guidance or an effective road map, associates' business-development activities tend toward occasional and opportunistic rather than proactive and strategic. Betting their future success on happenstance or providence won't cut it. "Hope" is not a strategy. They need a plan.

Since opening Fishman Marketing 20 years ago, I've conducted 300 firm retreats and marketing training programs. I've seen the exact same nervousness in associates at nearly every single firm, from Illinois to Istanbul. From Ghana to Gary, Indiana.

Lawyers and marketers alike kept asking for a simple, practical, and detailed guide that associates could follow—a step-by-step, year-by-year list of precisely what marketing and business development activities to undertake to help avoid inefficient floundering and increase the chance that they'll have their own business when they need it.

What follows is that guide.

It's become my most popular resource. If you have any comments or suggestions for improvements, please feel free to email them to me at ross@fishmanmarketing.com.

Good luck!

Introduction

As a new associate, your goal should not be to bring in work, but to master the skills you need to be an excellent lawyer and to put yourself in the best-possible position to successfully develop a pipeline of high-quality legal work *later* when you will be expected to generate work or create business opportunities.

To do that, your goal from the very beginning of your associate career should be to build a strong and productive network. Gradually and systematically, over time, you will want to build a tight 250–500 person network of people who hire lawyers, influence the hiring decisions, or refer business to them.

Few clients will hire an associate for a larger case or deal; you simply don't offer enough cover if a representation were to go bad. ("Wait, you hired an *associate* for this?!") Therefore, spend these important early years building your resume, reputation, and name recognition within a significant, specific target audience.

Note: In the longer term, the likeliest path to having a sustainable, portable practice is to become one of the go-to experts in a small niche industry or sub-subset of a larger industry; clients declare "industry expertise" to be among the traits they value most in their lawyers. Your goal shouldn't be "more marketing" but rather to become a member of the "automatic short list" for some type of representation.

For example, as a junior partner, a friend of mine developed a $2 million/year book of sustainable business just filing "small, Midwest-based securities-industry broker-dealer raiding lawsuits." (I discuss this niche strategy in greater detail below, under "Fourth- and Fifth-Year Associates.")

As an associate, focus on helping people, not looking for legal work. You want to be viewed as a knowledgeable, trusted industry insider, not a needy salesperson. Build a large number of close relationships following the steps below and you'll significantly increase the chance that you'll have your own clients.

In all your networking, remember, as a friend of mine once said, "It's better to be interested than to be interesting." Be interested in them and in facilitating their success, more than being the center of attention. Just because the stereotypic rainmakers are gregarious doesn't mean that's why they get hired. That just helps grow their network; they tend to get hired because they are good at listening, and finding ways to help people solve their problems.

As my father used to say, "When you're talking, you're not selling."

This list is extensive, but it's not intended to be all-encompassing or mandatory. You needn't follow every single step. If you don't want to give speeches, for example, if that's not your thing, that's entirely OK. Maybe do a little more of some of the other things. Just be intentional, deliberate, and consistent over time.

And if you're in a big hurry, then you need to compress the timeline. If you're starting your own practice or are at a smaller firm where you're expected to bring in clients right away, you have less time to develop your legal skills and market reputation. You'll need to get out there, meet people, leverage existing relationships, and find that critical business or industry niche that will give you something credible to sell (see "A Plea to Focus Your Marketing," starting on page 43).

A landmark study by my friend Dr. Larry Richard ("The Lawyer Types," *ABA Journal*, July 1993) showed that lawyers are in the 90th percentile for being sociable. The good news is, although you might be quiet, shy, and hate marketing, most of your competitors are the same way. Here's Ross's First Rule of Legal Marketing: "You don't have to be great. Just don't suck as bad as your competitors."

Marketing's not hard. It's just hard *work*.

First-Year Associates

MINDSET:

Become an excellent lawyer.

Your first priority is to learn to be a great lawyer; external marketing isn't important yet. Your only real proactive activity should be ensuring that you don't lose touch with the people you already know. Maintain relationships with friends from college and law school and any organizations you belong to. Create a reminder to make sure that you've had some contact with your chums once per quarter. Your future self will thank you.

This is the year you should create the basic platform you'll be working from over the next few years, the infrastructure you'll gradually expand over time:

☐ Join one local, state, or national **bar association** and get involved in one targeted educational committee within your practice area.
  o Meet your peers.
  o Learn your craft.
  o Invest in your profession.
  o Your long-term goal should be to chair a small committee during your fifth year of practice.

☐ Read your firm's website, internal website portal, newsletters, LinkedIn or Facebook pages, and other marketing materials to learn about its range of services and clients.
  o Read your senior associates' and partners' biographies and profiles as well, to learn about their practices and outside interests. This will come in handy later.

☐ Build your personal brand within your law firm. Focus on internal marketing by developing relationships with your firm's lawyers, both inside and outside of your practice area.
  o Also focus on getting to know the professional staff at your firm, they will be able to serve as a sounding board and guide to internal relationships.

❏ Do not spend your career eating lunch at your desk. Go out:

    o Once each week with a firm lawyer inside your practice area

    o Twice each month with a firm lawyer outside of your practice area

    o Regularly with friends and contacts

❏ Monitor your office visitor list.

    o Stop by and introduce yourself to the firm lawyers visiting from other offices.

    o If there is time and it's appropriate, ask to grab a coffee.

❏ Draft a detailed **website biography**, following the firm's format.

    o Update it regularly, especially when your practice is developing.

    o Ideally you should update it every time a matter you are involved with concludes, you publish an article or give a presentation, are appointed to a committee, etc.

    o Make it a habit that when you update your biography you also update the matters you have worked on in your firm's experience-management or knowledge-management system, such as Foundation.

    o Update it thoroughly at least every six months.

    o Be judicious in what you include. Delete all items from high school.

    o Be sensible regarding college activities.

    o Delete any *Who's Who* directory "honors" or other question-able accolades. See my blog post at *http://goo.gl/jWrQlY.*

❏ Build your network. **Create a mailing list** of friends and con-tacts, don't forget to leverage your firm's Client Relationship Management (CRM) system, you never know where your class-mates will end up. By participating in your firm's CRM program, you can leverage your relationship to help create introductions with

various technology tools your firm may use, such as RelSci. Opt for more, rather than fewer people, when deciding whom to add.
- o Law school classmates
- o Childhood, high school, and college friends
- o Former colleagues
- o Community association and professional club contacts
- o Parents of your children's friends and contacts through your children's activities

☐ Keep in touch with your existing network, leveraging both traditional and online tools, like:
- o Events, newsletters, holiday cards, breakfasts, lunches, drinks, phone calls
- o Social media, e.g., LinkedIn, Facebook, Twitter, Snapchat

☐ Before you engage in any marketing or social media, review
- o Your firm's social media policy
- o Your state's ethics rules governing the use of marketing, communication, and social media (generally Rules 7.1–7.4; see *http://goo.gl/JOhhF*)

☐ If you don't have a **LinkedIn** page already, create one. This will be your most-important social media platform.
- o If you *do* have a LinkedIn page from college or law school, do a thorough audit to ensure it is now professional.
- o Sanitize it so there's nothing a 65-year-old client or the most-conservative senior partner would find offensive.
- o Fill it out completely, including the Summary, Contact Information, Experience, and Education sections.
  - • Infuse it with your personality.

- o See "How to Draft a Persuasive LinkedIn Profile" in the Addendum.
- o Add a quality photo. No cropped, vacation, or wedding pictures.
- o Write in the first person with a friendly, professional tone.
- o Create a custom public profile URL. There are many simple explainer videos available on this topic.
- o No one expects it to be very long; you've only been a lawyer for a short while.
- o Review the privacy settings.
- o Check it weekly.
- o Post occasional relevant Updates, including thought-leadership pieces you have written.
- o It's easy to start by sharing or liking things that others in your firm or professional network have posted.
- o Remember, listening and engaging with what others post is as important in social networking as what you say and post.
- o Join your law school LinkedIn alumni group and your firm's LinkedIn group.
- o Consider starting a group for your law school graduating class.
- o Build your LinkedIn network; connect with friends, peers, co-workers, acquaintances, and classmates.
- o Regularly "Endorse" clients, friends, peers, co-workers, and prospects; it only takes a click. They'll typically endorse you back.
- o A word of caution with Featured Skills + Endorsements: When you receive an endorsement from someone for a specific skill, only post it on your bio if you have actual expertise in that area. Some state bar rules have restrictions on this.
  - o When in doubt, leave it off.

facebook

☐ If you don't have a **Facebook** page already, create one.
  - o If you do have a Facebook page from college, law school, etc., do a thorough audit to ensure it is now professional.
  - o Update your security settings.
  - o Hide the party photos, etc.
  - o Sanitize it so there's nothing a 65-year-old client or the most-conservative senior partner would find offensive.
  - o Keep it casual and sensible.
  - o Check it at least weekly, from home.
  - o Join your law school alumni Facebook group.
  - o Connect with your friends, especially those from law school.

☐ If you don't have a **Twitter** account, create one under your name.
  - o Check it occasionally.
  - o Build your Twitter network; connect with contacts and thought leaders.
  - o Post at least weekly on something relating to your job or interests.
  - o Re-tweet tweets that resonate with you.
  - o Consider utilizing Twitter as a listening platform to better understand clients, prospects, competitors, scholars, and more.
  - o Pay attention to what they are promoting, discussing, or commenting on. It can all be valuable.
  - o Follow people, companies, associations, and organizations within your legal, business, and general areas of interest.

Alerts

☐ Sign up for **Google Alerts** at *google.com/alerts*.
See video at *https://goo.gl/bAeQhj*.
- o For the Search Terms, use "[your name]" and "[your firm's name]" (in quotes).
- o Consider also creating alerts on friends, relatives, and prospects.
- o Drop them a quick email when you see them mentioned.
- o Even more powerful is a short handwritten note.
- o Reach out to your firm's library to identify other alerts and news feeds you may want to subscribe to.

☐ Develop a reputation for providing the highest-quality **client service**.
- o Remember, the profession is full of smart, technically skilled lawyers.
  - • Clients value lawyers who excel at communication, timeliness, and accessibility.
- o Keep clients regularly informed regarding the current status of their matters.
  - • Send them copies of all relevant correspondence.
- o *Always* call clients back promptly, ideally within two hours.
  - • Consider: if you have a sick child, how would you feel about a pediatrician who has an "All calls returned within 24 hours" policy?
  - • If you are unavailable (e.g. on a plane, in court, etc.), have your secretary check your phone messages regularly.
    - o Have him/her return the client's call.
    - o Explain that you will be unavailable until a particular time. Ask if they would like their call returned then, or if they would prefer having someone else address the issue sooner.
- o Give clients and prospects your cell phone number.

- They will appreciate the offer and won't abuse the privilege with late night or weekend calls.
- Consumer clients (e.g. divorce and criminal defense) are the exception. They *will* call.
  o Check your email at least once every night and daily on weekends.

☐ Always, always, *always* have **business cards** with you; you never know when you're going to meet someone who could later turn into a client or referral source.
  o The box of 250 cards gathering dust in your desk drawer can't help you unless they're with you when you need them.
  o Leave 75–100 in the box at work, then divide up the rest among all of your pants pockets, suit coats, blazers, jackets, overcoats, gym bags, purses, briefcase, backpack, suitcases, roller bag, and glove box.
  o In particular, put a thick stack in your suitcase, so you don't forget them when traveling.
  o To avoid embarrassing mix-ups, keep your cards in your left-side pants or jacket pockets, and cards you collect on your right side.
  o Watch my brief video at *https://youtu.be/rAA3291QWnQ*.

☐ If you're starting your own firm,
  o Find a way to connect with a senior lawyer—a mentor who can offer guidance, help teach you some skills, and throw you some overflow work.
  o Your initial clients will likely be your historic relationships.
  o You can find many practical new resources dedicated to this area online. Also:
    - Consider joining the American Bar Association's GPSolo group, at *https://www.americanbar.org/groups/gpsolo/*
    - Buy Jay Foonberg's popular *"How to Start and Build a Law Practice,"* at *https://www.americanbar. org/products/inv/book/227007931/*

Second-Year Associates

MINDSET:
Build your internal brand
and develop your network.

Your first priority as a second-year associate remains learning to be a great lawyer; marketing is still a distant second. Continue to focus on building your internal brand for excellence, efficiency, and teamwork.

❑ Stay in touch with your friends and contacts.

❑ Continue the "First-Year Associates" activities, above.

❑ Continue adding new names to your mailing list and to your LinkedIn and Facebook networks as you encounter these contacts.
- o Bar association committee members
- o Your peers within client companies
- o People you meet at networking functions
- o Alumni association contacts
- o Co-counsel and opposing counsel

❑ Join LinkedIn groups of the associations and industries you are involved in.
- o Pay attention to the conversations.
- o Learn who are the industry leaders.

❑ Read legal profession trade magazines, law-specific blogs, and online news sources to improve your technical skills.

❑ Volunteer for firm committees and activities when lawyer help is needed. It's a great way to raise your profile and get to know people in other areas of the firm. Also begin to volunteer to help with practice group activities such as writing up matters for rankings and awards such as Chambers.

❑ Volunteer to help firm lawyers or business-development professionals compile client pitches and presentations, to gain an understanding of the process.

Third-Year Associates

MINDSET:

Continue developing your external network, including relationships with your in-house contemporaries.

Start developing a toolkit of the soft skills that will become increasingly important to your success, e.g., an elevator speech, public speaking, writing or co-authoring articles or blog posts, and interpersonal communication skills to inspire confidence.

By now you're getting a better handle on your legal practice. Continue improving your technical skills, but you can begin to be more proactive in growing your network.

☐ Continue the First- and Second-Year Associates activities, above.

☐ Build your resume by participating more actively in your bar association within your practice area.
   o Volunteer for a committee and work toward a leadership position.
   o Write a brief article for a committee newsletter.
   o Give a speech on an area of particular interest.

☐ Increase your marketing efforts; devote time each week to a proactive networking activity, e.g., meals, sports, professional events, etc.

☐ Master a basic **"elevator speech"** (plenty of good how-to information is available online).
   o Tell people what you do in a memorable, personal way.
      • Avoid using jargon.
      • Talk about the benefits of what you do.
      • Keep it so simple that a child could understand it.
      • See my video at *https://youtu.be/SH4mjyvXZEI.*
   o In addition to your elevator pitch, have short answers ready to everyday questions such as "How are you?" instead of saying "busy" or "swamped," have an anecdote ready about a new matter you are working on or a new restaurant in town that you went to. Always remain upbeat.

☐ Learn to turn social contacts into potential business contacts.
   o This is a long-term process; it takes typically at least 7

to 20 touch points with a new contact before you begin to have a chance of getting hired.
- o "Active listening" is important.
- o Come prepared to ask well-informed questions about their business. Don't forget to leverage your firm's competitive-intelligence and knowledge-management tools.
- o Listen for opportunities to help them achieve their goals.
- o Find ways to help them become successful in their careers
- o Ask your Marketing Partner to bring in training on networking and working a room. Also check your local bar association for marketing lunches.
- o See my brief video at https://goo.gl/Bwq9ii.
  - • Networking is a learned skill. It's not difficult, but many behaviors are counterintuitive to most lawyers.
  - • Most importantly, remember that work is brought in by listening, not talking.

☐ Attend marketing training offered by the firm.
- o If the firm doesn't offer it, request it.
- o The leading firms are spending more time and effort on business-development/sales activities.
- o See the video at *https://goo.gl/4RxHNp.*

☐ Look for opportunities to develop new business from existing clients.
- o When chatting with your peers inside client companies, listen for new areas where they might need a lawyer.
  - • Did they mention that they were having trouble with an employee? They might need an employment lawyer.
  - • Did they mention that they were considering buying a new building, expanding into a new state, or developing a new product or service? Mention these issues to the partner in charge of the client relationship.
- o Follow your target clients' competitors to develop

industry intelligence and ask your peers thought-provoking questions about what their competitors are doing to gain insight into undiscovered needs.

☐ Read legal and targeted industry publications, print and online (continue through partnership).
   o Subscribe to blogs and follow Twitter accounts of leaders in these industries.

☐ Add select client and prospect names to your Google Alerts (e.g., "Fishman Marketing")
   o Use information you receive as a reason to contact, congratulate, or reconnect.

☐ Reach out to new lateral attorneys who join your firm.
   o Introduce yourself.
   o Develop relationships and become a helpful resource.

☐ Get to know your firm's marketing and business-development professionals.
   o They can be a great resource for you.
   o They often have valuable marketing opportunities to share. If they see that you respect them as professionals and value their advice and contributions, they're more likely to offer you the strategic perks that come across their desks.

☐ Update your LinkedIn profile.
   o Add organizations, volunteering experience, and honors and awards.
   o Add your top thought-leadership pieces to the Publications section and include a summary and the article URL.

Fourth- and Fifth-Year Associates

MINDSET:

Continue refining your legal skills.

Expand your network and build your external reputation and résumé.

Focus on client-service skills and interacting with clients.

Big-firm associates may transition to Senior Associate status.

Solos and small firm associates should be gaining traction.

Remember that providing the highest-quality technical skills and extremely responsive client service are essential elements of your firm's marketing to its existing clients.

As a fifth-year, you should chair a local bar association committee as a persuasive résumé builder. You may also seek to create a new one, to leap-frog the competition. Finding that I enjoyed marketing, I called the American Bar Association and became Chair of the ABA's national Marketing Legal Services Committee. (FYI, I was also the only member of this previously defunct committee. I invited my boss and quickly doubled the membership to two people, then invited a couple of friends and doubled it again to four. It looked great on my nascent Marketing résumé.)

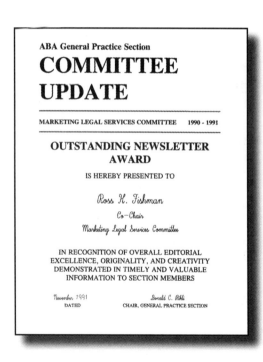

ABA General Practice Section

COMMITTEE UPDATE

MARKETING LEGAL SERVICES COMMITTEE   1990 - 1991

OUTSTANDING NEWSLETTER AWARD

IS HEREBY PRESENTED TO

Ross H. Fishman

Co-Chair
Marketing Legal Services Committee

IN RECOGNITION OF OVERALL EDITORIAL
EXCELLENCE, ORIGINALITY, AND CREATIVITY
DEMONSTRATED IN TIMELY AND VALUABLE
INFORMATION TO SECTION MEMBERS

November 1991   *Donald C. Pehli*
DATED   CHAIR, GENERAL PRACTICE SECTION

A Plea to Focus
Your Marketing

This is the time to starting focusing your efforts more narrowly, particularly toward an industry group or sub-specialty practice niche. See the videos at *https://goo.gl/fKR7AA* and *https://goo.gl/QtmJTT.*

Here's the larger point: When the next recession hits, I wouldn't want to be just another smart and skilled but generic and easily replaced generalist. I'd rather be the one who offers more, a skill or expertise that your firm can't find in every other associate in your class.

You also become much easier for others to cross-sell if you have a unique expertise that the partners can remember when in conversations with prospects. *"You manufacture bicycles? [Or build prisons, or license offshore oil-rig technology, or...?] One of our corporate associates has expertise in that area!"*

For new grads who are starting their own practice, it'll be a while before clients will be hiring you purely for your legal talent. But if you're the lawyer who knows their industry best, you'll have an advantage over those who may have superior legal skills, but don't have your business insight. The fastest way for a newer lawyer to gain client-development traction is to find that specialty niche.

For example, I probably know more about Industrial Tire Manufacturing than just about any lawyer in the world—it's my family business. My father and grandfather designed and built tires for heavy equipment, like underground mining crawlers, loaders, etc.

Growing up, the specs of new tire sizes and the composition of tire fill was typical dinner conversation. As a child, I played with toy Caterpillar forklifts. I vulcanized rubber for my fifth-grade science-fair project. I worked in the factory in high school. I've flown in the Goodyear blimp.

That is to say, I take for granted an insider's nuanced understanding of this narrow little industry. But practicing as a litigation associate, it never occurred to me that some group of clients would have found that unique knowledge to be valuable. Instead of marketing "general commercial litigation to Chicago-area businesses," I should have been marketing my tire-industry expertise to companies like Goodyear, John Deere, Caterpillar, the rubber importers, and chemical manufacturers.

They would have valued having a lawyer who knew their industry as well as they did. But it simply never occurred to me that I possessed any uniquely useful information. Now I know better.

It's not enough to specialize in the obvious industry sectors like real estate, health care, construction, financial services, or insurance— they are simply too broad. You must be more precise and find a niche within them (e.g., FCA litigator in health care, D&O liability in insurance). You will also find opportunities in smaller, more-defined and obscure areas where you have existing experience, interest, or contacts. Think in terms of focusing on Pest Control rather than on Banking. Not Transportation Law but Transportation of Infectious Biological Material. See the video at: *https://goo.gl/3GWNQa.*

Consider segmenting it further by geography and/or the particular type of company or size of matter. The answer might not be obvious now; just look for it and recognize it when it comes along. It takes at least a few years to build this, so start being proactive in this regard beginning around your fourth year.

For example, at Fishman Marketing we have developed marketing initiatives supporting lawyers and firms who targeted niche industries or practices including these:

- Ad valorem property tax cases in Chicago
- Alabama pest-control companies

- Backyard barbecue propane tank explosions in Colorado
- Boy Scout abuse personal injury cases in Chicago
- Bridge-and-tunnel construction companies in Florida
- College-athletics coaches in the SEC
- Cuban personal injury cases in South Florida
- Defending the Chicago police in Taser-related cases
- Divorce cases for Iranian immigrants living in Canada
- Estate litigation in Vancouver
- Ghanaian law firm seeking inbound referrals
- Global aircraft and railcar finance under U.S. law
- Health care lobbying and intellectual property
- Health care software licensing contracts
- Multi-generational family businesses
- New York companies doing business in Israel
- Northern California agriculture industry
- Oil and gas companies in Louisiana
- Personal injury appeals
- Personal injury cases for St. Louis Catholics
- Surfing lawyer in Southern California
- Trucker DUI defense in northern British Columbia
- Upstate New York forestry and timber regulatory

Examples of the marketing materials we designed for some of them are on pages 51-56.

Considerations in identifying the niche or industry to target include:

- Did you grow up in a family business?
- What was your college major?
- What hobby, passion, or special skill or interest of yours would clients value?
- What job did you have before law school?

- What's hanging on your walls or sitting on your credenza?
- Where do you or your spouse have an established network?
- What do you know that other lawyers don't that would benefit some category of clients?
- What type of law do you practice?
- What are you seeing as growth trends within your practice?
- Think through your list of friends and family members. Are several of them in one particular industry or niche?
- *Fill out one of the handy "Niche and Industry Marketing Checklists" in the Addendum.*

To help you identify your narrow niche, visit a public or law library to review a printed copy of Gale Publishing's multi-volume *Encyclopedia of Associations.*

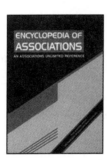

☐ Browse through the easy-to-use 25,000-association directory to identify the best trade groups or professional associations serving your target industry.

    o   Seek a 500- to 1,000-member national association with an active local chapter.

☐ Call them to learn more about their members and request a membership kit.

☐ If the membership includes legal-hiring decision makers, consider joining the group.

☐ Don't worry if the members are junior or mid-level professionals; build relationships with them when you're both starting your careers. They'll be able to start choosing their own lawyers when you're in a position to get hired.

☐ Validate that group with your contacts who know it.

Once you have selected the organization or association, your ultimate goal is to become one of the "usual suspects" in that group—a highly visible, friendly, helpful, active contributor. Spend a couple years just learning about the industry and the association members.

☐ Attend at least 8 out of 12 monthly local chapter meetings per year.

☐ Network regularly and actively; get to know everyone.

☐ Keep the conversations focused on *them*.
   o Remember the 80/20 Rule of Communication:
      • You should spend 20% of the time talking, mostly asking interested, insightful questions about them and their businesses, and 80% of the time listening.
   o Remarkably, studies show that the more they talk, (1) the smarter they think you are, and (2) the more they like you!
   o Be actively interested in them.

☐ Be helpful; offer advice and assistance.

☐ Join a committee and follow through on any assignments or responsibilities.
   o People will judge your legal skills based upon how you perform as a volunteer. Do you meet your deadlines and commitments?

☐ Do not seek work or sell your firm, or you will be shunned as an <ugh> "vendor."

Try to understand "why they buy," not "how to sell to them."

When I got started in marketing, our profession's organization was the national Legal Marketing Association, with 300 members. Working in-house as a large firm's Marketing Manager, I was one of the few lawyers in the group. I discovered that I had something to contribute, that my knowledge of the law was helpful, so I began writing some articles for the local chapter and giving some speeches. They were well received, and I began to be invited to write and speak nationally. I was surprised to discover that I enjoyed it.

Within a few years, I realized that without even trying, I knew almost everyone in the entire national association. More importantly, they knew *me* as a helpful, trusted member of the legal marketing community. I'd dedicated my external communications activities toward a relatively small and finite group, just 300 people—half the size of my high school graduating class.

Over time, I just kept writing and speaking and networking. Writing and speaking and networking. Writing and speaking and networking. I later was invited to become the LMA's vice president, which further increased my visibility. None of this was especially complicated or challenging; it was just the basic blocking and tackling that anyone can do.

Eight years later, when I left the law firm to go into consulting and needed to get hired by law firms, the LMA had grown to 3,500 members, and I found that I knew most of them, or at least they'd frequently read my articles and seen me speak. I had a national network of thousands of prospects who knew what I did and had a generally positive impression of me and my expertise.

I'd built this network entirely inadvertently. And with some basic planning and regular execution, absolutely anyone can do this on purpose.

Leasing aircraft doesn't have to be done on a wing and a prayer.

Is this:

☐ a family pet

☐ the beneficiary of your father's entire estate

 MacLEAN Estate Litigation

bcfamilylaw.ca

Peace of mind for parents with the most vulnerable children.

Prescribed by Drinker Biddle lawyers.

More Activities for Fourth- and Fifth-Year Associates

☐ Identify a **client development mentor**, ideally a young rain-maker who's invested in your future and can help answer questions and provide guidance and support.

☐ Learn about your clients' and prospects' companies and industries.
- o Regularly read industry websites, publications, and blogs.
- o Conduct online research periodically to stay current on their issues and needs.
- o Browse company websites regularly, especially sections like "About Us," "What's New," and "Press Releases."
- o Follow them on social media.
- o If your firm has a Competitive Intelligence team, work with them to leverage firm tools like Manzama Insights to learn more about your target companies and decision makers.
- o Create a Google Alert for each company and important decision maker.

☐ Update significant matters you have worked on in your experience-management or knowledge-management system. Also work with your marketing and business-development professionals to learn about the key details that help matters stand out in rankings, awards, and RFPs and include that information in your write ups. These activities will help raise your profile with others in the firm who might not have had the chance to work with you yet.
- o See *"How to Write Persuasive Case Studies"* in the Addendum.

☐ Notify your firm's marketers of significant cases and/or transactions you are involved in, or aware of, for media and public relations purposes.

☐ Tweet at least weekly on issues relevant to your narrow area(s) of interest.

☐ Write an article for a legal or industry publication or blog on new issues, trends, or precedents relevant to your area(s) of interest.

  o Ask to include your photos(s), which will enhance your networking and brand.

  o Invite a client to co-author it with you, as a nice value-add.
    • Most likely, you'll do 90% of the work.
    • Frame a reprint and give it to the client over a follow-up lunch. It'll hang on their office wall, with your face on it.

  o Another option is to use the article as an opportunity to get a meeting with a valuable prospect.
    • "I'm writing an article on XYZ and I need to quote an expert on this topic. Could I interview you for the article next week over lunch?"
    • This is a great way to meet important executives.
      o This is just the first contact. Remember, it could take a dozen more before they would potentially be willing to send you some business. It's a marathon, not a sprint.

  o Continue regularly through partnership.

☐ Give a presentation to a legal, industry, or community association or at an in-house client seminar. Carefully select the topic, using it to support your chosen niche or specialty practice.

o Your goal shouldn't be to simply give a nice, educational speech—it's to give the speech that the audience will remember next week.

o Aim high and strive to give the best darn speech at the entire conference, the one every attendee will be talking about.

o If you enjoy speaking, seek to build a reputation as a strong presenter; there aren't many lawyers who can be both substantive *and* entertaining.

o Strong presenters build their reputation quickly.
  - Even if yours isn't the best speech, the attempt will improve the quality significantly.
  - You're likely to get invited back next year, and word will spread around the industry.

o **Audiotape and transcribe the speech**, or use voice-recognition software.
  - This single transcribed speech can be repurposed into dozens of different-length articles and blog posts for various audiences.
  - Edit the transcription into dozens of tweets and social media updates.
  - Professional editors can do much of this work for you, if you have a marketing budget.
    o *"Here's the 10,000-word transcription of my speech. Please edit this into 100 tweets, 10 blog posts, one 5,000-word article, three 1,250-word articles, and five 500-word articles."*
  - Get professional presentation training. Public speaking is a learned skill.
  - Rehearse, rehearse, rehearse.
  - Ensure you get videotaped, and review it afterward. It can be mortifying to watch, but it's the

best way to improve.
- Continue presenting through partnership.
- Invite a client to co-present with you (as a nice value-add).
  - o Most likely, you'll do 90% of the prep work.

☐ Use this speech as the foundation of a wide range of material you will reuse, repurpose, and republish, spreading it across the Internet. See the video at *https://goo.gl/gf9eHF.*
- o With a smartphone and portable tripod, videotape your presentation.
  - Upload the entire speech to Vimeo.com.
  - Trim the speech into as many quality 2- to 3-minute snippets as possible, and upload each of them to YouTube as individual videos, once every couple weeks.
  - Use narrow, detailed keywords and buzzwords in the captions, tags, and descriptions so Google will index them thoroughly.
- o Upload the PowerPoint slides to slideshare.net.
  - Create a thorough, detailed SlideShare profile.
    - o Google highly ranks SlideShare profiles in name searches.
    - o Connect the SlideShare slides to your LinkedIn profile.
- o Post links and updates of your videos and slides to LinkedIn, Twitter, Facebook, and other social media accounts.
- o If you're committed to speaking, hire a video editor to turn your speeches into a demo video.
- o For example, my speaker video is online at *https://www.youtube.com/watch?v=G1Abh_uo6LE.*

☐ Collaborate with your firm's Marketing Department professionals.

❑ Learn how to produce and leverage client information and competitive intelligence.
- o There's an abundance of valuable information available.
- o Use your firm library as a resource to help access competitive-intelligence information.
- o Smart attorneys and firms understand how to leverage the power of critical information.

❑ Continue adding to your social network with friends and close professional contacts.

❑ Continue to engage in at least one face-to-face marketing effort per week, such as breakfast, lunch, dinner, drinks, sports, social event, seminar, conference, or association meeting.

❑ Consider hiring a professional presentation consultant.

❑ Offer to host a meeting at the firm for a group you're active in.

❑ Volunteer to help organize or host your law school's fifth-year reunion.
- o It's a great way to stay visible with hundreds of referral sources nationwide.
- o Repeat for subsequent reunions.

Sixth Plus-Year Associates

MINDSET:

Start demonstrating that you're ready for partnership.

Stay in touch with and provide value to clients.

Share successes with contacts.

Enhance external profile and increase visibility.

Work with a practice-group leader or mentor to set annual business-development goals. Continue the activities listed above, supplemented with additional activities:

☐ Meet with contacts at other professional-services firms (accounting, financial services, real estate, management consulting, public relations) to identify strategic-partnership opportunities such as co-hosted events, client teams, and referrals.
    o Follow-up to events and meetings is critical.

☐ Unless your practice area is driven primarily through lawyer referrals (e.g., litigation boutique, appellate, personal injury, divorce, patent, admiralty), reduce your bar association activities and instead surround yourself with prospects, rather than competitors.

☐ Work toward a leadership position in your selected industry association.
    o Consider running half-page ads in the industry publication, if
        • You would be the only law firm advertising there, and
        • You can make the ads visually interesting enough to truly stand out. See *https://youtu.be/jqy-x8GiE1E.*

☐ Use technology to help grow and stay in touch with your network, e.g., blogs, Twitter, LinkedIn, etc.
    o Keep your platform narrow and *focused*. The world doesn't need another general "Litigation" or "Real Estate" blog or Twitter feed.

☐ Request professional LinkedIn Recommendations, as appropriate.
    o Write Recommendations for clients and prospects.

❏ Engage in at least two face-to-face marketing efforts per week.

❏ Ask your partners and business development professionals to allow you to join them on pitches and client-assessment visits when appropriate.

❏ If your small firm pays for martindale.com or lawyers.com, seek both Peer and Client Ratings/Reviews. *(http://research.lawyers.com/lawyer-ratings.html)*

> James R. Figliulo Lawyer Profile on Martindale.com
> www.martindale.com › Figliulo & Silverman, PC › People ▾ Martindale-Hubbell ▾
> ★★★★★ Rating: 5 - Review by Peers on Martindale.com
> **James R. Figliulo** Profile by **Martindale**-Hubbell. Find **James** R. **Figliulo** contact information, experience and credentials, peer review ratings etc.

❏ Visit clients on-site at their offices, factories, facilities, or stores, at no charge.
  o Many rainmakers consider client visits to be the single most-important, most-effective marketing tool available.
  o Dress appropriately for the location (suit, or jeans and work boots).
  o Tour the plant, meet employees.
  o Prepare for this visit. Research the client before you go, understand what your firm is doing for them holistically as well as what other firms they might be using for things like litigation or transactions. Ask insightful, educated, well-researched questions.
  o Become more familiar with their industry's legal and business issues.
  o This is critical: You are there to enhance your relationship and learn how to represent them better; DO NOT SELL.

❏ If you enjoy Twitter, follow the journalists who cover your practice area or industry.
  o Engage with them occasionally.

- Build relationships with journalists who may ask you to act as a resource for articles.
- Offer to provide expert commentary on cases or current legal developments.
  o Others who follow those journalists may follow you too.
    - Twitter is a geometric, not linear, platform.

☐ Look for Ross's forthcoming PR book, *"The Ultimate Public Relations Handbook for Lawyers,"* available on Amazon in mid-2019.
  o Learning basic PR skills isn't especially difficult.
  o Lawyers who understand how to use the media to their advantage can expedite their marketing success.
  o Two brief "PR for Lawyers" videos:
    - A 3-minute clip discussing what PR is and how it differs from other types of marketing, at *https://youtu.be/JE9wkgK7AHY*
    - A 10-minute clip discussing what makes something newsworthy, at *https://youtu.be/yylgCJpZ4i8*

☐ Talk to your marketing professionals regarding the analytics from your client alerts and blog posts and how you can use the information for business-development purposes.

☐ Write multiple versions of your elevator pitch.
  o Quick version: One or two sentences
  o Medium version: One to two paragraphs; an expansion of your quick version
  o Long version: An expansion of your medium version; can include example clients, representative engagements, and other relevant information
  o Alternative versions: Create customized versions of your elevator pitch for different audiences

General Mindset

Always remember, whatever your job, always do more than is expected. Get to work a bit earlier, stay a little later. Pay attention to how the partners are dressed. Ensure that your shoes are shined, and your clothing is neat and clean. Show that you care, that you take this important profession seriously and are dedicated to doing your best for the firm and its clients.

Clients can't often tell whether you're doing a good technical job, but they can tell how well you're treating them. Communicate regularly. Meet your obligations and deadlines. Be responsive–don't make clients wait to hear from you. Try to return every call and email within two hours and never let a call or email go unreturned overnight.

Treat every person at the firm with the utmost respect regardless of their age or title. Learn the names of all of the receptionists, secretaries, clerks, and messengers. It's not only the decent thing to do, people notice. It matters.

And understand that law can be a difficult and stressful career. We work long hours on intellectually and emotionally challenging projects for clients who may seem demanding and unappreciative. It is essential to take care of yourself. Eat right, get enough sleep and exercise, and spend time with your friends, family, and hobbies. Volunteer for a charity. Ensure you have a vibrant and fulfilling life outside of your practice, as well.

Conclusion

If you follow this checklist, over time you should find that you have developed a significant network of contacts you can turn into clients. Moreover, you will have laid the foundation for a successful career, one that is fulfilling personally, professionally, and financially.

Remember, once you identify what you love to do, find a way to bring that into your practice. If you do, you may spend your time until retirement leaping out of bed every morning absolutely passionate about your profession, your career, and your success.

Good luck!

ADDENDUM

NICHE AND INDUSTRY MARKETING CHECKLIST: LONG VERSION

Niche/Industry Marketing© Worksheet for Lawyers

What industry or niche specialty practice should you focus on?

Target companies must be appropriate to the size of the firm:

- What's your specialty niche?

- What type work do you want more of?

- Are there people/industries you particularly enjoy?

- What types of companies are most likely to hire you?

What skills, interest, or passion leads to an appropriate target?

- Something interesting/unusual about you?

- Previous job/career providing insight?

- Family business you worked in?

- Spouse's business you have contact in?

- Existing client providing industry experience?

- Previous big win/case study to get you started?

- Personal connections to give you a leg up?

- A hobby that engenders useful insight?

Select *one* industry group or trade association.

Browse through the *Encyclopedia of Associations (see page 47)* and select a little-known, niche-oriented trade or professional association upon which to focus your marketing efforts—ideally a national organization with a nearby local chapter where you can focus your monthly networking activities. Surround yourself with *clients*, not competitors.

- You must be active, visible.

- Attend monthly meetings.

- Join the membership committee.

- Work to leadership position.
    - o   Committee chair
    - o   Conference chair

- Focus most of your marketing activities on this group.
    - o   Networking, research, biography, articles, speeches, public relations, ads, etc.

Some ways to focus your practice, a health care example:

- **Geography:** "National" is usually too broad. Define a narrower geographic region.

- **Size of business:** Focus on a certain segment of the business (e.g. just small or large hospitals).

- **Type of business:** Subset of a larger industry (e.g. ambulatory care facilities).

- **Injury type:** Focus on a certain type of injury (e.g. punitive damages or emotional distress).

- **Practice area:** Specialize in a narrow area (e.g. kidney dialysis or anesthesiology).

- **Or a combination:** Select two among the list (e.g. radiology cases in small hospitals).

"So, what do I do after identifying some likely organizations?"

- Contact them; the information is in the *Encyclopedia of Associations*.

  "I represent companies in your industry and would like to learn more about your association. Do you have a local chapter?"

- Request membership information.

- Learn about pricing, benefits, member demographics. Are they your target prospects?

- Analyze the conference schedule, magazines, and website.

So, what's the plan?

- "We don't accept [vendor] members."
  "I can help members avoid trouble, protect themselves, save money...
- Write articles for magazine, newsletter
- Preventive-law monthly column
- Local/national conference speeches
- Network monthly at local meetings
- Advertise

Summary

Focusing your marketing clarifies your message and identifies how to use the standard tools most efficiently and effectively:

- Website
  - *Micro-site or blog* directly on point.

- Networking
  - *Finite audience* to meet.

- Research
  - *Specific industry* to learn about.

- Biography
  - *Tailored experience* to describe.

- Social media
  - *Add to LinkedIn bio.*
  - *Twitter* can establish expertise with the media.

- Brochure, print or electronic
  - *Targeted* to group's needs.

- Articles
  - *Focused message* is easy to discuss in print or on blogs.

- Speeches, Newsletters
  - *Interested audience* and a narrow topic.

- Public relations, quotes
  - *You're the expert,* so reporters need you.

- Advertising
  - *Inexpensive placement* in targeted publications or online.

NICHE/INDUSTRY MARKETING CHECKLIST: SHORT VERSION

Seek to identify one or more narrow niches in which, if effectively marketed, you could use to build a successful, focused practice. Where can you become a market leader? This form seeks to focus your thoughts regarding where to start.

Consider specific industries, narrow market segments, target communities, geographic regions, sub-practice specialties, and/or areas of narrow expertise. Avoid broad, traditional headings like Health Care, Real Estate, Insurance, Construction, or Financial Services. In what niche do you have the threshold level of expertise and limited law firm competition?

1. What narrow niche or industry should you consider targeting?

2. Identify any other firm lawyers who have experience in the target area.

3. Briefly describe your interest or expertise for this niche or industry.

4. Identify one or more existing clients or contacts in the targeted area.

5. Identify the best trade associations or similar organizations serving the target area, if you know (or look in Gale Publishing's *Encyclopedia of Associations*)

6. Identify any lawyers or firm(s) who would be your primary competitors.

7. How might you or the firm distinguish yourself from competing law firms in those areas?

INDIVIDUAL MARKETING PLAN: LONG VERSION

Describe Your Personal Marketing Goals for [year]

I. Developing Your Network and Reputation

Clients perceive professional activities like writing, speaking, and bar- and industry-association activities as indications of your knowledge and skill. Ensure clients know about your activities by sharing through the firm's marketing outreach, and posting to social media.

A. Networking

Networking is the foundation of client development. Build a network of the *right* contacts. After a thorough analysis, *precisely* identify the most likely sources of new business for the practice you are trying to develop—your "target audience." Next, find out which industry or trade associations they belong to and which meetings they attend. Then join those organizations and *work toward a leadership position.* You can't get business if the people who hand out the business don't know, trust, and respect you. This is a critical, *long-term* professional-development activity.

I will actively participate as a member of:

❑ **Industry or Trade Association(s)** In which *industry* would you like to develop contacts? What groups do your clients belong to?

❑ **Bar Association(s)** These help professional development and build a strong resume. For business-development purposes, it is better to be the only lawyer in a roomful of potential clients than sitting among other lawyers. Allocate your time carefully. As a young lawyer, select one bar association and work toward a leadership position. *Get active and visible!*

Association/Section	**Committee**
_____	_____
_____	_____
_____	_____
_____	_____

B. Supporting Activities

Certain activities support the firm's marketing. Some are included below.

❑ I will create or regularly update my CRM lists and LinkedIn connections.

❑ I will create or regularly update my biography and social media profiles.

❑ I will help draft or update written promotional materials (e.g. blog posts, social media, newsletters, etc.) targeting the following department, practice area or industry:

_____

❑ I will commit to creating or helping update my matters in the experience-management or knowledge-management system.

❑ I will commit to creating or helping update a list of representative cases or transactions.

❑ Other, describe:

_____

_____

_____

II. Developing Existing Client and Prospect Relationships

It is important to focus much of your marketing efforts on maintaining and expanding existing relationships.

A. Strengthening and Expanding Existing Client Relationships

Roughly 80% of a firm's new business comes from the top 20% of its clients. Lawyers should commit to strengthening, enhancing, and expanding these top relationships. The primary focus is to learn more about their businesses and industries, strategic business goals, and legal needs so that you can provide more informed and useful counsel. An added benefit of this enhanced understanding is that it positions you to identify new business opportunities. As the General Counsel of a Fortune 500 company said, "If you're not willing to take the time to learn about me, you do not really want my business." List the two current clients you will work to strengthen the firm's relationship with.

Existing Client's Name:

_____

❑ **Company Research.** It is important to have current information about firm clients. To learn more about their company and industry so that I can serve them better, I will review their website, including the "What's New" section. I will leverage firm resources to learn more about my clients. (see *www.google.com/alerts*)

❑ **Client Visit (5th-year associates and up).** Within 6 weeks, I will volunteer to visit the client's facility, for free, to learn more about them and invest in the relationship, so that I can understand their business and enhance our service. I will tour the facility, and meet their people at all levels, but I will not market to them in any way. Instead I will learn about their goals, personnel, products, and operations.

- ❑ **Attend Trade Conference.** This year, I will offer to go with the client to his/her trade association conference at no charge, to learn more about his/her business and industry.

- ❑ **Read Industry Periodicals.** Within two weeks, I will view online and/or subscribe to (and read) the client's and competitor's trade journal(s) or blogs, to learn more about his/her business, industry, and jargon. The client would be delighted to learn of my interest and inform me of the best publications to read.

- ❑ **Write Industry Article.** This year, I will co-author an article or blog post with a client.

- ❑ **Make Conference Speech.** This year, I will arrange to speak at the association's next conference on a topic of particular relevance to this industry, co-presenting with a client if possible.

- ❑ **Attend Client Meetings.** This month and every two months thereafter, I will offer to attend the client's internal meetings, at no charge, to learn more about them, and offer advice on accomplishing its goals.

- ❑ **Entertain Client.** Every two months, I will entertain this client for a meal, event, etc.

- ❑ **Present In-House Seminar.** I will offer to conduct a free seminar on a useful topic.

- ❑ **Add to Mailing List.** I will ensure that this client and its key personnel are on our list.

B. New Client Development

Although it is a less-efficient way of bringing in new business, developing new clients is still important. List below one non-client target you will seek to develop business from during the coming year, and any additional support that you need to help you accomplish this.

Prospect's Name:

❑ I will conduct current company research.

❑ I will seek to visit the prospect's premises within six weeks.

❑ I will attend the prospect's industry/trade association meeting this year.

❑ I will view online and/or subscribe to (and read) the prospect's relevant trade journals and blogs within two weeks.

❑ I will co-author with a prospect a short, industry-focused article this year.

❑ I will seek to co-present with a prospect an industry association speech this year.

❑ I will volunteer every two months to attend the prospect's internal meetings.

❑ I will entertain this prospect every two months.

❑ I will seek to present an in-house seminar to this prospect.

❑ I will add this prospect to the mailing list.

III. Additional Resources

What would help you succeed with your marketing?
List the top 5 in order.

(1 is "least important" and 5 is "most important").

———— Training in how to network or work a room better

———— Training in how to focus my marketing to achieve better results

———— Training in how to be more effective in new-business proposals and competitions

———— Training in advanced client-service strategies

———— More individual instruction/coaching

———— Assistance from colleagues (describe:)

———— Institutional support and leadership

———— More knowledge of firm capabilities

———— More time

Describe:

_____

_____

_____

_____

_____

_____

_____

INDIVIDUAL MARKETING PLAN: SHORT VERSION

MY 100-DAY INDIVIDUAL MARKETING PLAN

Clients: In the next 100 days, I will focus on increasing our involvement with the following existing clients (list clients and indicate the type of contact you will make with each client):

1. _____

_____

2. _____

_____

3. _____

_____

Prospects: In the next 100 days, I will initiate contact with the following organizations who are not currently clients of the Firm (list prospects and indicate the type of contact you will make):

1. _____

_____

2. _____

_____

3. _____

_____

Meetings: I anticipate having the following new-business meetings (face-to-face meetings with potential buyers) during the next 100 days (list):

Current Clients	**Prospects**

Positioning: In the next 100 days, I will conduct the following "positioning/broadcasting" business-development activities (speeches, articles, seminars, mailings—general passive marketing activities):

1. _____

_____

2. _____

_____

3. _____

_____

Proposals: I anticipate developing the following proposals for our services during the next 100 days (list):

1. _____

_____

2. _____

_____

Other: I will conduct the following "other" business development activities during the next 100 days:

Hours: I plan on devoting _____ hours per week to business development during the next 100 days.

Evaluation: The ways I will evaluate my business development efforts at the end of the 100 days will include: _____

_____

HOW TO WRITE
FOR THE INTERNET
AND ENHANCE YOUR SEO

Biographies, LinkedIn pages, blog posts, and other online material can and should be used to elevate your rankings on search engines like Google (called Search-Engine Optimization, or SEO). We know roughly what Google's algorithms are looking for, which makes it possible to draft your materials in a way that uses this information to improve your results. Although there are no guarantees and the rules continue to change, leveraging this information and staying current on the trends and updates improves your chance of being found by your target audience of buyers and referral sources.

Fundamentally, Google tries to connect each search with the specific pages on credible websites that seem to best match that search. Therefore, when drafting the pages you would like ranked highly by Google, write from the perspective of a prospect seeking that information, working backwards from the specific Google searches they would conduct. Consider the exact terms they would use in the search box and use that same language in your online materials, like websites, LinkedIn, and other social media.

These days, sophisticated users are conducting longer, more complex searches, including narrow specialty areas or identifying particular types of contracts, clauses, phrases, or statutes. They include the name of the city, state, or province which means you should also if you want to persuade Google that your page is highly relevant.

Here is one of the least-known, but most-important pieces of information in this area: There are no "actual" Google search results—results differ on every computer. Google basically knows who and where you are, and tries to tailor the results to be most helpful to what you're probably looking for. This means that your search results will be very different from someone conducting the exact same search down the hall or in a different city or country. It's why when you search for "Plumber" you'll see plumbers in your local geographic area and not from Paris or São Paulo.

This reality can lead to biased results and a false confidence in your success. When you conduct a general "organic" search, your firm may receive a high ranking because Google knows your personal search history and your previous interest in that firm. But a more objective or disinterested searcher, like a prospect searching from a different city, might not find you on Google at all.

It's not unreasonable for sophisticated purchasers of legal services in the US to look for a skilled law firm in a far-flung jurisdiction by searching online. They might not do that for a major practice area in a major US city (e.g. "Boston litigation") where they can easily find a direct, in-person referral. But when seeking a professional in a smaller or less-well-known jurisdiction, Google searches become a useful option. But a firm buried on page 3 or lower will be out of competition. And that's a missed opportunity.

WRITING AN SEO-ENHANCED PRACTICE-AREA PAGE

- Describe the type of issues, services, questions, and tasks you deal with everyday.
- Engage your target audience by writing your text from your prospect's perspective. Let's consider an Intellectual Property group:
  - o The firm may proudly offer a "full-service IP practice," but hot prospects rarely search for the terms "IP" or "intellectual property."
  - o They more commonly seek "trade secret policy" or "registration of trade marks" or "licensing agreement." Therefore, those are the terms you should use in your practice pages as well.
- Refer to relevant statutes, landmark cases, seminal doctrine.
- Drop in the name of your firm instead of simply referring to "we."
- Include specific geography—the cities, states, provinces, and countries you serve.
- Mention that *"[Name of your firm] represents clients in the following counties:"*
  - o List the counties or judicial subdivisions by name. Be careful, if the list is too long, Google may think that you're trying to inappropriately "pack" these terms, and penalize you.
- List the articles that you have written.
- If you are writing for your practice group, add: "Contact [name of attorney] at [phone number] or [email address] for more information regarding our [practice group] Law practice."
- List the names of the attorneys in the practice group, and link each name to their respective profiles.
- Add examples of work you may have done that validates the answer, e.g. client names, attorney names, cases won, and relevant statues.
- When referring to cases or statutes, you may add the complete title or link directly to them.

WRITING AN EFFECTIVE INDUSTRY-GROUP PAGE

Industry pages offer the opportunity to mix keywords that are difficult to impart in the text relating to your professional profile or practice area. This includes geographic terms (e.g. Detroit, Motor City, Michigan, Midwest), techno-legal terms (such as "molder's liens"), and statutory references (statutes, agencies, cases, and conferences).

Here is an example of a strong industry page prepared by a Detroit-based client:

CONTRACT AND SUPPLY CHAIN COUNSELING PAGE

With our roots in the Motor City and decades of combined experience, our contract and supply chain-counseling team at [Firm Name] understands the risks, costs, and challenges of the automotive and manufacturing supply chains. This in-depth knowledge enables us to provide some of the world's largest manufacturing clients with practical and detailed advice regarding how to understand, mitigate, and allocate the risks associated with selling complex automotive and non-automotive components, assemblies, and systems in a relentlessly competitive environment.

We help our clients with:

- Supply chain contracts and long-term agreements
- Terms and conditions of purchase and sale
- Pricing and material economics contracting, planning, and training
- Tooling and molder's liens and asset protection
- Supply chain risk/allocation gap analyses
- Warranty and warranty share agreements
- Intellectual property and trade secret agreements regarding manufacturing assets and know-how

Our team also helps automotive manufacturing companies understand and comply with the applicable safety and regulatory rules and regulations affecting their products, including:

- National Highway Traffic Safety Administration (NHTSA) rules, compliance and reporting
- Understanding and managing voluntary and mandatory recalls
- TREAD Act and Early-Warning Reporting planning and compliance
- Training, planning, and counseling for automotive manufacturers new to the United States

You will notice that any of the topics on this page could be live links that open to new pages that would speak to such topics in greater detail—you can start developing those pages when you have time.

Finally, one last word on the makeup of this page: you can also link certain of the items to other parts of the site. For instance, "TREAD Act" could link back to (i) a specific practice page; (ii) the profile of one of the attorneys who specializes on the application of this statute; or (iii) an event, conference, or article that speaks to this subject. These "lateral links" can create significant improvement both from an SEO and user-experience perspective.

Similarly, when drafting your profile, consider the references and links that can be made to specific industries.

WRITING A GREAT WEBSITE BIOGRAPHY/PROFILE PAGE

One of your most-important marketing tools is a persuasive website biography. Most prospects will check out your bio before deciding whether to meet with or hire you. Website visitors are looking to identify an attorney with specific skills and experience, and match that against their particular needs.

Profile

While there are several ways to organize the content on a biography page, we suggest that you present the information as follows:

A. High-level summary

In 50 to 100 words, summarize your key skills. Refer to your position in the firm, reputation in legal circles, and standing in an industry. This is also where you can reinforce the main attributes of your firm's brand messaging with a personal message.

This short paragraph can also serve as your signature abstract that you would use whenever there is a reference to you outside the website (in a program where you are speaking, an article you wrote, a video where you are featured, etc.)

You may also list your most-recent article, blog post, conference, or presentation—only one such entry is necessary here.

B. Career Highlights

In bullet-point form, list your top five highlights: this is where you are "packaging" yourself in terms that are relevant to your target clients and prospects. Where appropriate, link back to specific practice-area or industry pages on the site. In addition to your general experience, be sure to detail any particular expertise you have in the narrow specialties, niches, or industries you have selected as your marketing targets.

The career highlights should also be replicated in your LinkedIn profile.

This is also where you refer to your practice area(s), and responsibilities in such practice areas.

C. Particulars
- Education
- Publications: list articles, presentations, blogs, videos (with full title) and if possible an abstract of the subject dealt with in such material. All such material should be linked to the full version of the publication. Add a statement that you would be happy to send copies of the articles.
- Bar / Court Admittance
- Memberships
- Awards / Honors
- Social Platforms: addresses and links
- Community involvement with links to landing pages on the site for any association where you hold a leadership position. This is where you have a chance to articulate your commitment to such cause.

D. Complete résumé
You can offer your visitor the opportunity to review or access a comprehensive listing of your résumé. In such a listing, you should provide full descriptions of relevant matters, such as the complete name of tribunals where cases are heard, cited cases, deals, and press clippings.

Photo
Your headshot/photo should be recent and produced by a professional photographer.

Coordinates

The following basic information should also be made available:

- Name
- Office phone
- Cell phone
- Address (if multiple offices)
- Vcard
- Name of assistant
- Practice area(s)
- Email
- LinkedIn Profile Link

DRAFTING A PERSUASIVE LINKEDIN PROFILE

This memorandum will serve as a checklist of essential items that should appear on your LinkedIn profiles.

1. List Your Full Name

Do not use abbreviations. Married women who changed their name should include their maiden name as well.

2. Display a Professional Photo

There are reasons why some people don't want to display their photos, but this is a social networking platform. Not displaying your photo raises more questions than provides answers. Ensure that it is a professional, high-quality photograph. LinkedIn is not Facebook; do not use cropped group, vacation, or wedding photos. No props or artistic effects. Express your personality, but err on the side being more conservative. Here's the LinkedIn photo of Joe Fasi, whom I write about on pages 96-97. Doesn't he look solid and trustworthy? Don't you already want him as your lawyer?

3. Have a Professional Headline That Properly Brands You

In the space underneath your name is your "Professional" or Profile Headline. It will appear in search results next to your name, as well as next to any questions you ask or answer. It is, in essence, your elevator pitch in a few words. Do not simply put your title and firm name here: this is the place to interest anyone who finds you in a LinkedIn search result to learn more about you.

Think more in terms of "Raleigh Property Tax Attorney" or "North Carolina Family Law," rather than "Associate, Smith & Jones LLC."

4. Have Something Relevant and Timely in Your Status Update
The Status Update is about showing that you are still relevant in doing whatever you are doing. Going to an event? Share it. Attending a conference? Share it. Read something interesting that is relevant to your brand? Share it. Use your Status Update to show your relevance, and try to aim for a once-a-week update. You don't want someone visiting your profile and see a Status Update that is months old...

For those who enjoy writing, LinkedIn is an ideal platform to push out your articles.

5. Display Enough Work Experience... with Details
Your LinkedIn profile doesn't need to be a resume. One simple sentence summarizing what you did is enough to ensure that a potential reader understand the role that you had. Job descriptions provide you the perfect opportunity to pepper your profile with narrow, search engine-friendly keywords that will help you get found. For example:

> Amber concentrates her practice in the area of litigation, with a primary emphasis on litigating large commercial disputes. She regularly represents financial institutions, corporations, limited liability companies and individuals in contract, corporate, shareholder, U.C.C. and fiduciary disputes in all of the federal and state courts of North Carolina, including the North Carolina Business Court.

6. List Your Education

Put education details on your profile. What did you achieve at a certain school? Honors, awards, or activities? Mention them.

7. Get Some Recommendations

The LinkedIn "profile completeness" algorithm requires that you receive three recommendations in order to get to 100%. This is not critical, but is useful. Do not be embarrassed to ask friends who know you well to recommend you; it's a well-understood part of social networking today. And when you've done something particularly great for a client, that's the optimal time to sheepishly tell them that "the firm's marketer insisted that we ask for some LinkedIn recommendation." That is, blame "Marketing" if it'll make you feel less awkward to ask; your client will understand. Email them the link, to make it easier for them. And of course, it's only polite to recommend them back!

8. Acquire Connections

If you're on LinkedIn you should be networking. Connections are also important to help get found in the huge LinkedIn database. Rule of thumb? Multiply your age by 10 and that is the *minimum* number of connections that you should have. Join some relevant practice and industry groups and connect with the members you know. Start with your firm, any previous firms you've worked for or jobs you've held, and your law school class. Connect, connect, connect.

9. Your Professional Summary is *Essential*

The Professional Summary section is the first thing people will read, right after your headline. Don't just dump the first 2,000 characters of your standard resume into your LinkedIn Summary. This is how you will introduce yourself to your professional contacts, and future clients, referral sources, and employers. This is the most-important professional social-networking platform, so why not spend a few minutes introducing yourself? This is the place for you to tell your own story, in your own voice, typically with a bit more personality than your firm's website bio.

Devote the time necessary to make your Summary truly great. Admittedly it can be difficult to write this way about yourself, so get some help if necessary from a professional writer, or perhaps an old friend who aced that college creative writing class.

Here's a LinkedIn profile that I wrote for my friend Joe Fasi, one of the nation's top trial lawyers. Joe's a kind, modest guy, and he wins complex ten-figure cases because juries like and trust him. It's just 333 words long, but see if it helps you start forming a generally positive impression of him and his technical skills:

> Most people know the movie "The Maltese Falcon." I am not the Maltese Falcon, but I am from the island of Malta and speak fluent Maltese. I also like to speak to jurors, and do so often and in cases with large damages at stake. I've tried over 100 jury trials to verdict, defending complex cases with enormous exposure against sympathetic plaintiffs.
>
> I haven't counted up my precise win-loss record, but a client recently asked me "how the heck I keep winning all these cases." I wasn't exactly sure how to respond to that, but I smiled and thanked him for what he intended as a compliment. Thinking about it later, I suspect the answer might partly be that I don't get involved in the games that many litigators like to play. I don't play puerile hide-the-ball tricks. I'm aggressive, but honest and reasonable. I want a fair and just resolution and, if a plaintiff wants my client to pay a lot of money, they better prove that they're darn well entitled to every penny of it.
>
> In post-trial research, juries have universally said that they liked me—they felt I approached the trial with decency and integrity, and trusted me to help them get at the truth. This is particularly important because it means I become the face of the faceless corporation. I've helped level the playing field.
>
> Fewer and fewer large cases actually go to trial. When they do, I defend them, nationwide, for companies that are among the most skilled and strategic purchasers of legal services, including manufacturers, pharmaceutical, and tobacco.

I typically handle cases as the lead trial attorney, getting hired at the outset to resolve a problematic dispute or lawsuit. Some companies use me as a their "go-to attorney," parachuting me in on the courthouse steps, either to support an existing trial team, or simply take over and handle the trial, especially the large or challenging cases.

Specialties: Product Liability, defense of nursing homes, and professional/medical liability.

11. Claim Your Personal URL

When you sign up to LinkedIn you are provided a complex "Public URL." You can customize and simplify this when you edit your profile with a couple simple steps. If you have a common name, make sure you claim your URL before others do! My LinkedIn URL is *https://www.linkedin.com/in/rossfishman/*. It's simple, and yours should be too. You can then include your abbreviated LinkedIn link on your email signature, business card, and everywhere else you go online. A quick Google search will find short videos detailing the simple steps.

12. Add Your Website(s).

You can add up to three website links. You will want to link to your blog and you may want to link to a page of any attorney directory where you're positively referenced. You should make a title for each website link—instead of having your firm name as the title, use something like "North Carolina Personal Property Tax Advisor."

13. Join Relevant Groups

You should join Groups that are relevant to your areas of interest and expertise, get active in the discussions to help meet people in your growing professional network, build your brand as a helpful and knowledgeable member of the community, and start connecting with the members as mentioned above.

HOW TO WRITE PERSUASIVE CASE STUDIES

Among the most persuasive components of a lawyer's written marketing arsenal is a current collection of case studies (also called "war stories"). Clients regularly comment that direct, relevant experience can be the decisive factor when selecting their attorneys for a particular case or matter. It is important to your marketing efforts to draft and maintain an updated collection of these examples as you go throughout your career.

In determining whom to hire, prospects are thinking, "Don't tell me that you *can* do something, show me that you've already *done* it successfully." This information is important to have in your online biographies, and for use in competitive new-business materials.

Attached is a simple, fill-in-the-blanks form to expedite the collection of this data. Before creating your own process, remember to leverage the professional staff at your firm to find out if there is additional information that you should collect or if there is firm-wide experience-management or knowledge-management system or process in place. You may choose to either fill in the blanks and start from there, or simply dictate the information following the Sample Summary format in the example shown below. With a little practice, you can dictate new case studies in just a minute or two.

LITIGATION CASE SUMMARY FORM

Case Facts:

1. The simple case caption was: _____

_____

2. Client name: _____
   ❑ Plaintiff ❑ Defendant

3. The court/jurisdiction was: _____

_____

4. The *total* amount at issue was: $ _____

5. Client description - revenues, industry, etc. [e.g. $250 million pharmaceutical co.]: _____

_____

6. Relevant issues/allegations of complaint:
   [e.g. fraud, RICO, breach of contract]: _____

_____

7. The names of the firm's legal team: _____

_____

8. Full description of outcome (settlement, dismissal, jury verdict etc.): _____

_____

_____

Case Highlights:

9. IMPORTANT: Describe how the client benefited specifically by your work (e.g. how did you save them time or money, develop an innovative strategy or tactic, etc. that another lawyer might not have considered):

_____

_____

_____

_____

_____

_____

Sample Litigation Summary

This is a short, easy-to-read format that provides all the necessary "who, what, where, when, why, and how" information for your prospects. Remember to use plain English and short sentences, simplifying it as much as possible, targeting an eighth-grade reading level. It's not that your targets can't comprehend big words and complex sentences, just that when reading text online, they prefer not to.

Par-D, Inc. vs. U.R. Safe Company

We defended U.R. Safe, a middle-market manufacturer of smoke detectors, in a $5 million product liability, fraud, and wrongful death action in Vermont state court. The plaintiff alleged that a defective smoke detector manufactured by our client caused the fire which destroyed the plaintiff's liquor store. Following a month-long trial the jury returned a verdict in our client's favor on all counts in just 45 minutes. The case was settled on appeal, setting an important precedent in the field of liquor store conflagrations.

CORPORATE CASE SUMMARY FORM

Deal Facts:

1. Client name: _____

   _____

2. Other parties involved: _____

   _____

3. The *type* of transaction was: _____

   _____

4. The *total* amount of the deal was: $ _____

5. Client description - revenues, industry, etc.
   [*e.g.* $250 million pharmaceutical co.]: _____

   _____

   _____

6. The names of your legal team: _____

   _____

   _____

7. Description of the deal: _____

   _____

   _____

   _____

Deal Highlights:

9. IMPORTANT: Describe how the client benefited specifically by use of our firm (e.g. how did we save them time or money, develop an innovative structure, *etc.* that another firm might not have done):

_____

_____

_____

_____

10. May we use the name of this client in our marketing materials?
❏ Yes   ❏ No

Sample Deal Summary

This is a short, easy-to-read format that provides all the necessary "who, what, where, when, why, and how" information for your prospects. Remember to use plain English and short sentences, simplifying it as much as possible, targeting an eighth-grade reading level. It's not that your targets can't comprehend big words and complex sentences, just that when reading text online, they prefer not to.

Acme Incorporated

We represented Acme, a $500 million mail-order company engaged in the manufacture of roadrunner-catching devices, in a coordinated series of sophisticated financings totaling $250 million. These include its public offering of $135 million of senior subordinated notes and $115 million of senior secured discount notes. Proceeds from the note offering and the term loans, along with proceeds from a prior private placement of common stock, will be used to design and construct a new jet-propulsion backpack to be marketed to desert coyotes.

NOTES

NOTES

NOTES

Ross Fishman

Ross Fishman is one of the legal profession's most popular marketing and ethics CLE keynote speakers and trainers. Often characterized as both highly entertaining and educational, Ross's presentations draw on his experience as a litigator, marketing director, and marketing partner, inspiring lawyers at all levels.

A Fellow of both the College of Law Practice Management and the Litigation Counsel of America (LCA), Ross has branded 200 law firms worldwide and has written 300 bylined articles. He received the international Legal Marketing Association's first peer-selected Lifetime Achievement Award, and was the first marketer inducted into the LMA's international Hall of Fame. Subscribe to his marketing blog at *fishmanmarketing.com/blog*.

A 1986 member of the federal Trial Bar (N.D. Ill.), Ross received a B.A. in Speech Communications, *cum laude*, from the University of Illinois, and his J.D. from Emory University School of Law.

**Contact Ross directly
to book him for your
associate-training program,
firm or partner retreat,
or marketing-training
or Ethics/CLE programs,
at ross@fishmanmarketing.com.**

Acknowledgments

The Ultimate Law Firm Associate's Marketing Checklist was initially based upon my experience and memories working as a fresh-faced litigator at a progressive firm that offered marketing training to associates. I drafted the first 4-page version of this checklist 25 years ago as an in-house marketer, to support the industrious associates who eagerly sought advice.

I truly appreciate the countless suggestions I've received over the years from lawyers, marketers, and administrators, many of which I adapted to enhance the quality of the material. And during each new iteration, I sought input from industry peers who selflessly volunteered their unique perspectives. I am grateful to the experienced marketing, business-development, and technology professionals whose expert insight informed this current version. My sincere thanks go out to them:

Katherine Hollar Barnard
Chief Marketing Officer, Shook, Hardy & Bacon

Jeanne Hammerstrom
Chief Marketing Officer, Benesch

Gail Sobha Lynes
Senior Director, Business Development, Morgan, Lewis & Bockius

Rachel Shields Williams
Senior Manager, Experience Management, Sidley Austin

And a very special thanks to **Michelle Benjamin**, Fishman Marketing's extraordinary Creative Director, for her contributions to every single Fishman Marketing project over the past 15 years, including designing and laying out this book.

Finally, I am grateful to **Fishman Marketing's valued clients** who have trusted me over the years to educate their esteemed attorneys on the marketing techniques presented in this book.

Need More Books?

Small orders are available on Amazon.com.

Purchase 10+ copies at a bulk discount
by contacting Ross directly
at ross@fishmanmarketing.com.

Connect with Ross

LinkedIn: https://www.linkedin.com/in/rossfishman

Twitter: @rossfishman

Subscribe to our Blog

Go to fishmanmarketing.com/blog

FISHMAN
MARKETING

Ross Fishman, J.D.
CEO

Blogs:
fishmanmarketing.com/blog
lawfirmspeakers.com

Twitter: @rossfishman
LinkedIn.com/in/rossfishman

1356 St. Johns Avenue
Highland Park, IL 60035 USA
+1.847.432.3546 [847.HEADLINE]
ross@fishmanmarketing.com

fishmanmarketing.com